RESTORATION

CHRISTINA PUGH

Restoration

POEMS

TRIQUARTERLY BOOKS

NORTHWESTERN UNIVERSITY PRESS

EVANSTON, ILLINOIS

TriQuarterly Books
Northwestern University Press
www.nupress.northwestern.edu

Copyright © 2008 by Christina Pugh. Published 2008 by TriQuarterly Books/Northwestern University Press. All rights reserved.

Printed in the United States of America

10 9 8 7 6 5 4 3 2 1

Library of Congress Cataloging-in-Publication Data

Pugh, Christina.
    Restoration : poems / Christina Pugh.
        p. cm.
    Collection of poems, some previously published.
    ISBN 978-0-8101-5206-9 (cloth : alk. paper)—ISBN 978-0-8101-5205-2 (pbk. : alk. paper)
    I. Title.
PS3616.U35R47 2008
811.6—dc22

2008024164

♾ The paper used in this publication meets the minimum requirements of the American National Standard for Information Sciences—Permanence of Paper for Printed Library Materials, ANSI Z39.48-1992.

CONTENTS

ACKNOWLEDGMENTS

Grateful acknowledgment is made to the editors of the following publications, in which some of these poems first appeared:

Atlantic Monthly: "Rue Family"

Cimarron Review: "Journey in a Circle"; "Reconstruction: An Emblem"

Crab Orchard Review: "Embouchure"; "The New Retina"; "Windy City" (as "City in the Air")

Memorious: "Loan"; "Cicadas"

Ploughshares: "I Shall Not Want"

Poetry: "Retro"; "Twenty-Third"

Poetry Northwest: "Sebald's Dream Props"; "Seeing In"

TriQuarterly: "Mercurial (Soap, Glass, Skull)"; "One Thousand Cranes"

I would like to thank the Ucross Foundation for a residency in 2005 and the Illinois Arts Council for an individual artist's fellowship in 2007.

"Twenty-Third" was featured on *Poetry Daily* on February 16, 2006.

My thanks to those who provided commentary and advice at various stages of this manuscript's development: David Barber, Reg Gibbons, Anne Winters, John Skoyles, Bruce Bennett, and Christian Wiman.

And my deepest gratitude to Richard DelVisco, Lisa Petrie, and Walter and Sybil Pugh.

RESTORATION

Dream Work

Chords at Night

The stereo was playing
its Canon in D,
but *ritardo* unraveled
the bindings of the melody—
I heard the music of a book asunder:

each step of the wedding walk
now crawl stroke through mist,
now searchlight
in the ancient swamps,
while nether fish
electrified the ocean's pit,
and still the woodwinds tuned
and tuned.

Shredding, shredding: the music.

And beside me, the living
skin and breath,
the body in its deep canals;
and in me, the pictures
and the sounds: a torn rib lodged

to cordon off the dig,
and the chitter of their buried
alarms. And I crawled beneath
the bridge of music—
and tried again
to hear them raking ash
on ash.

September 2001

Musical

I had to teach them middle C,
that stop in the ocean
of keys: the first clear note
before anyone can cleave
sound from sound;

how to tread water
when your vision
resolves into two-tone,
slate pressing blue on the horizon,
and your small legs
ebb in the foam;

how to find the C
when the whole room breathes
and waits for your fingers
to trail the keys now
suddenly identical,
a whiteness no arithmetic can heal—

but when I turned to address
the loss of the middle,
the keys began
to school into sculpture,

swirled as a single scallop
of light: Vasari's *disegno*
trembled and formed,
as if to lend my new voice
something of its frequency.

Journey in a Circle

Ask again later,
my dream might tell me
if it spoke
as an eight ball,
blinking words
in a single eye.
But dreams
have no busy signal,
just the white light
of interference:
a radio
gruff with static,
varnishes of stars
on the TV screen.

So maybe again
tonight when I sleep,
I'll follow
the freckled man
acting out his exile:
a stealthy Tom
or Jerry in the glare—
pillaging a bay
of gilt spines,
then tapping
his conductor's baton;
or we'll motor
side by side
through the Belgian green—

where I'll look to my hands
and sorrow,
*I know nothing
about Beethoven;*
the river has never,
even once,
met my eyes.

Stitch

—Then the painter, carpenter, and God
correspond to three kinds of bed?

—Yes, three.

—PLATO, *REPUBLIC,* BOOK X

Infinite, the seat of dreaming,
issued from a trinity of beds:
the photograph, the bed upstairs,
the unimagined glinting
in a vacant lot—the seed
always fashioned at the outskirts
of what we can conceive.

I wonder how we're yoked
to the airborne form;
do blueprints yield
the forests of our rest,
Douglas fir and juniper
and soft needles
to cradle my head?

Imagine a carpenter
building the sky.
He'll extract a slat
from a liquid frame,
then ply a bed from cloud,
gleaned like Eve
from that immanence, the rib.

Down alleys, in stairwells,
his ghost-bed subsists,
flickering and fathering
our loneliness—that longing
for the angle and the sphere.
You'll feel it most
in the third remove,

the photograph, when fireflies
light on mosquito nets,
in snowdrifts fenced
by a headboard: a bed
can levitate as ice
or milk, and a man
still skirts my dream

like starfish—sinuous,
implacable,
his pressed double-
breasted suit
stitched from the blankets
I burrowed in
as I fashioned him.

Retro

That's me
in the smallest frame,
walking the dog
through the rebuilt

library, taking him
off someone else's hands.
It's been years
since I've held a leash,

but now I'm tugging
at that sheath of noise
and darkness underneath.
What's clear to me now

is you in the carrel,
where you've been sitting
and reading for days,
then the soft incline

of your neck—
the leaning stack
of leather and crumble;
and soon I'll see

the bark won't wake you;
neither would my voice
like this, or this:
you need

to take care; look,
the sky has changed
from cloud
to star.

Blue Window

Let's not ask how it was made—
this swan in a blue window,
swimming in snow. It's the word beneath
that moves me most: *crepuscular;* musty
frills from another century:
the Sylphides' dandelion slips,
a swan queen's arabesque *penchée*
draped one beat behind the music,
her left hand trailing
in that wake—and now, again,
I'm lost among the audience, the dancers.

My faith in you, in us, is only
half-formed, ghosted as that swan
in the dusk and ice; it lives with me
at night in single digits,
dropped vowels, the shards
of my sleep's jigsaw song—
not the way a dancer's *grand jeté*
scores the air with what the muscles know.

I understand that faith is always partial,
that it limps—that if I believe in gods
or parse a soul, I'll have to live
alone before technology,
there in the old myth country,

my selves in sheaths both black and white:
Odette and Odile, her four eyelids
glittering, because the slowly lowered head
means more than virtuosity:

the artifice begun at the barre
ends with the curtsey called *reverence,*
when the soul tries on letters
and sees itself windowed in each name.

Reconstruction:
An Emblem

Hide walls in an aqueous atmosphere:
a house you could hold

like a conch to your ear,
as if to sound the murmur

your life lost after the flood,
to listen for a pulse inside—

then it opens, the cotton door
waterlogged with cadmium and ochre,

and there's the old canvas
in the corner where you'd left it,

but with new mass:
the portrait anchored in more shade

than you'd ever had the skill
to invest, revealing a face

like a field in three-quarters light:
dirt and blossom

and all the integrity
you'd ever wished

your own skin to hold—
until *I made this?*

breaks from your mouth,
words in a language

that suddenly
you've never heard before.

A Boy, Listening

If he has not acquired them in his present life, is it not
clear that he had learned them at some other time?

—PLATO, *MENO*

This species of smile
could not have come
from watching, from
learning how:

it belongs
to his great-
aunt, who died
before she met him:

all the waiting
blooming in the face;
the eyes made
smaller, and flashing

just a fraction
of the teeth,
as the self fleetly
pours into the other

voice it hears:
in daily conversation,
a listening so generous
and strange—

not the feature
living on, I'm seeing now,
but habit; and this boy
has it: I'd believe

the old woman
appeared in his dreams
were she not
extinct in my own

bed at night;
I believe
she'd still shimmer
in that well—

but it's empty now,
and I have to know
who taught us:
how did you learn

to round your left
shoulder, to speak
fluent German
when you sleep?

Sebald's Dream Props

If I have to know a white room,
let it be a courtyard
where stems of parasols
lean in the soil,

snow dressing
and shining their ellipses,
and each rose print
iced out: blooming coin

or Linnaeus's riddle,
they'll lean
beneath the pediment
or plinth.

Then fold one leaf
as a page in my fingers,
and I'll test
the silkworm's

plush act, neither
stratagem nor bole—
but a dense smooth trail
the body fords

before the lake
stars through: pitch
for an oar,
a darkness borrowed.

Loan

And then your own page,
loaned in prefatory light:
the print dissolves
into corners, letters
loosened at the borders—

and you read as the aviator
reads, tracing the sleeve
of the Chesapeake,
wandering a blaze
over Broadway at night:

you the prime mover,
who'd dipped in the foam
circling your ankles,
and washed, and wrote
it all as if on water:

miles above a dust basin
deep in the continent's
plexus, you felt
a bitter stream scar,
trickle on the land.

World's End

A stand of iris rises as an island in the grass,
and I've stopped to track it over my shoulder—

shock-still, as if this petaled creature could startle
at a twig's crack, while stunted monarchs

light on weeds, certain in their mapping,
glazed with a sliver of frenetic; and can it be

that every dreamed clock has lost its hands,
here in the season of allegory? No longer a fire

or a slough enameled in Despond,
the end of the world is a strip of sand

fording two brother bodies of water,
and the sense you left your story at home.

Bindery

You had bound
the book yourself,
as if this

were a dream and I
the imaginary
author;

no longer
the Japanese
paper of the cover:

you'd poured
a plaster wall, enceinte
for the pages,

set the title in stalks
above a wooden
decoy of flowerpot—

densest vessel
for my words,
now yours

as you've sewn
and dressed them:
I'll dream

four new windows
in my house:
then knock

on the gate
and see if someone answers.
The sign translates

as *private garden,*
but I stand there
rehearsing what to say:

I used to live here.
Do you mind
if I look around?

Paris, 1950

So how can we dance
when neither of us
knows: the fox-trot
before my time
and yours—

but we've sprung limbs
from the trunk
of one tree,
and I answer you
with a murmured

circumflex—
we're nothing
but address, keen
address:

all night,
umbrella skirts
agitate around us,
and that old

woman in the corner
feeds me
lines: you are not
you gaunt you,
but still we step,

and I press:
let me dance until
the officer
contracts us one from one—

Shard

When the dream
was winnowed,

one phrase stayed:
our bodies, black

beside the blinking cursor:
a phrase to equal two:

a phrase I had never
spoken to you,

that I'd send you now,
to your screen.

In all our language,
yours and mine,

there never was
the story of our bodies—

parted, or wanting,
or not knowing.

And I was afraid.
But I felt

the two words
lay you down,

I felt my two words
marry us together.

Chamber of Commerce

Before you wrote me
the check
in the chamber,

I'd held you close,
your spine
loose beneath my fingers,

rippled
to the quick
of your black

dress: signaling
that someone
lay alone

at the foot
of a near hill,
fallen in the lush

street corner:
someone whose glasses
were broken, and more teeth

gone—someone
I'd loved
and wanted

to help—
who wore black,
too: but in his eyes,

his hair;
who'd no longer know
the face above the hand

stretched out
to him
when I did—

and I did:
and then was his bier
sward or tar—

Padeuteria

I had fallen
asleep in the sunlit
room   the only sunny
room in the house

and I dreamed
you were talking:
Well, and don't
you see, your voice

rising as in clear
discovery   (*Fact*
is the sweetest
dream)   your hands

in transport   to drape a large
book   an atlas
its jacket as an ocean
several pages

marked   I wept unashamed
ruined   in that small
public   *O to be*
in your classroom one

more time was what
I said   it had been
eight years   I didn't
know what a well

(and unknown
arms closed
around me)
though earlier

that day   it is true
I had wept
for the departure
of ink paper pen

and later   had read
padeuteria   in some
illustrious
glossary

          for Jonathan Aaron

Choose

Then, behind the door,
a flock of black skirts
at the barre,
milling like traffic
on a city street (the small
cyclones of 14th Street),
solemn as the rush
of strings tuning:
but they are children,
I told myself—
too many
for this paucity of wings.

Looking for Mother

If I heard castanets
as I slept,
how could it be
you who played them:
Irish girl, your flushed
face freckled—

but I was raised
up, stepped
to the sound
the dark wood
clapped above my head;

and if I once heard
footsteps in my sleep,
they too
were wooden
on the floors:

no shoes
you ever owned,
but then it rustled
and I knew you,

I knew you
like a mist over water;

if I wore a ring,
it had to be yours,

though I wondered
how it came there
on my finger—

delible as snow—
beveled glass
or beryl: the spindrift,
the ocean
and the foam.

Drown

Bill Viola, *The Messenger* (1996)

Whiter and more fluid
than any lover watched
underwater, his limbs
slow as hair
streaming weightless

as grass, he bubbles
gravely forward,
filling the screen
with the eyes
and beard of an apostle.

I want to look away,
because his air tank
and flippers
are missing; but now
he refloats his path

backwards, a pendulum
in increments,
the jeweled floor
suspending him
in lumens,

his head pooling
like voices
silvered into sonar,
until I can't tell
a mouth from a horn

from an IV drip—
here on the moon's
nearest channel,
the most pristine
of the deeps,

where the lost
mark time, splitting
the difference
between sleep
and a walk on the water.

Twenty-Third

And at the picnic table under the ancient elms,
one of my parents turned to me and said:
"We hope you end up here,"
where the shade relieves the light, where we sit
in some beneficence—and I felt the shape of the finite
after my ether life: the ratio, in all dappling,
of dark to bright; and yet how brief my stay would be
under the trees, because the voice I'd heard
could not cradle me, could no longer keep me
in greenery; and I would have to say good-by
again, make my way across the white
California sand and back: or am I now creating
the helplessness I heard those words express,
the psalm torn like a map in my hands?

Synesthetic

Leave me
only the caul
to wear,

and I'll revert
to the etches
cracked

above my crib
in the sunlit
ceiling;

I'll lie there
gathering
the grains

of drained
and primal
flowers: tumbled

geranium,
wax begonia
filling halls

summoned
by numbers—
sixties, seventies,

each ordinal
another turn
in the colorless

hothouse walk:
how near
old age felt then,

how near to me
in bed,
in corridors:

when night
kept one hand
in the light,

I counted steps:
now feint, now slow
processional.

My First Name

It gleams in the ilex
after winter,

or inks
a bridal gown with tea.

It measures a hummingbird's
frequency,

the slow arc
of arms in third arabesque.

When I lift up my hair,
before I wind it.

The umbel, the pebble trail,
the cloudburst:

that was my name,
before they named me this.

Parable

I didn't meet you at the Coliseum last night
in moonlight, the way we'd planned. I left you
tapping your feet and tagging scraps
of constellations, there in the crumbled
ancient seats; I left you overhung by clouds

and orphaned by night shouts. As I walked
the rank *vie,* waiting for a stranger's eye to fire
(a firefly: zephyrs of a black streak,
then grim *serenitas* when the moment passed),
I heard lilies clamor in their boxes—

cars slicked, and baked stucco steamed
beneath the street lamps, smoking out
all I imagined of your sentences, your sad
repartee; and the faith I knew you both had,
lighting on the ruins, that I'd come.

That then there'd be two sets of breasts,
four deft hands to braid his gray
braid down. That the three of us would live
in a land of hanging baskets,
sound the creak and whistle on the porch.

That the three of us would marry,
each with our own gold rings and our maiden names.
Mine would be *Tuber,* yours *Preen;*
his, *Ell.* But there I was in the night street,
swimming in the crowds, shepherding

my one and only name—
and sheltering from both of you,
running from the new world we'd planned.
In gaslight, the skins began to gleam
around me—and then I saw the topiary bird.

Two Beds

Why, again, did I need to come
to both your beds?

Why did you desire it?

I wanted to be
a small purse of fevers,

all the sweets compacted.

Instead the minutes
break against my mouth;

I need to trace each vowel
gone to seed, each

skin, each curvilinear.

My voice
has clattered into fractals,

as the rain beat on Hopkins—

and so I have to marble

the tulip's cup,
storm the delphinium. I need

to leave myself:

imagine me
alive, with no sentience.

Parable

I had murdered according to orders: counted
my steps, then gentled the barrel
hard against my breastbone.

I fired. Then stood and waited
for the first spurt of the wound—
for my legs to give,

and all the papered birches in the forest
to murk—when suddenly I felt the sun
sharpen on my shoulders,

and, terminal, I tried to yoke it there:
raveling a knot of light and skin; stepping
delirious upright.

The Dig

This
is the question
that was put to me:

If you had let
x = y,
and that
was your lot,

who
was x
and who was y?

I knew this had to do
with growth,
an increase
in skin:

with strands
of DNA
or storms in the larynx
before words.

How to solve for *x*
when chiasmus
is only the beginning—

the most
eloquent of ciphers?

And it
too is a form—

how shall I know
what spliced me,

what strove for me
and through me,

the waters

that glistened
me and in me

all the length
of that canal:

how can I know?

I may still
find a way
under all the weeds of words,

somewhere in the rift
between shape
and fluid,

transparency and terror.

Will I never
know the way
the letters

use me
and have used me—

Three-quarters
of an x
is a y:

now a portal
to someone else's dream.

Embouchure

What are these dreams: tough, lyric,
mosaic; moving, if they move,
in the manner of the husk
or the transitive: a fin lifting
in the water, or now the accordion's
reduction. In the dream I'm alone
with a voice that cannot sing
or stutter, and shards of the story
clatter as porcelain.

If I try to row my mother
to the open sea, I'm locked
before mountains, my hand cut
by a cascade's knife. The falls
tear me from the open. I have to lie
still in the canoe, to map with my burned
eyelids or the compass of my toes.
My dream is a cripple. And we won't
make it back before nightfall.

II

Case History

Notes for Dora

On Freud's *Dora: Fragment of an Analysis of a Case of Hysteria*

I

After the first floor of scilla
drained the grass of its early green,
I saw the landscape clear
and sculpt:

water was poured
into brick basins,
and dark blades of nymphaea rose.

Lotus had also risen from the water,
the hard hull of its pod
a nest of holes.

Dwarf pines ranged on a hill,
and a bridge was thrown to an island.

A rash of poppies grew
on that incline—gold, orange,
fire. And foxglove,
digitalis, with the mouth of infection.

II

The antiquities stared
when you crossed the doctor's study:
Osiris. Winged victory.
And chlorophyll,
hoary in its way.

Dim populace:
they loosened
your syntax
as you sat with the doctor,
ironing out the lining of your dream.

Your reticule was small
as a cigarette box.

When you spoke, the doctor
pried each noun
from its casing,
so the pearl eardrops trembled free.

III

Like many girls who saw the doctor,
you'd loved your father.

Years before, his retina
detached:

he floated in the sighted world,
saw gauze along the ore
the light let in.

I refuse to let myself and my two children
be burnt for the sake of a jewel-case.

The doctor watched your fingers
moving in the reticule.

IV

As soon as I was outside I woke up.

You'd dreamed your house burned,
you told the doctor—

a document charred
from flame to ash.

You spoke of your pulse;
how long it took to catch your breath.

Your mother wanted her jewel-case.
Your father, to save his children.

The jewel-case is a tin box
smaller than your hand.
Look inside:

a crash of buttons and snaps,
some silk-covered, some bone—
then a tether of glitter, rough to the touch,
the color of mink and water.

V

The box smelled of cigarettes.
The ocean was television.
The smell is California.

I wake in early morning
to the pleas of birds. Later in my life,
the world is again littoral;

there are fewer scraps to take
from the shore, but sometimes a glass shard
smooths and nests in my hand.

VI

A father's house is a seashell, watered by the ocean's din.
Listening, you moved
among the rooms.

But it didn't take long
for the world to lash you open:
the world of the man and woman,
K and K.

You'd seen the woman's white neck
and hands, the man's moustache,
and each sent a different song
through you: catarrh;
the fugue of sickness.

At the lake, K embraced you.

Cumulous and birdsong.

Against the dense back of the sky,
you only saw the sky.

I see now that the body
can twin,
will separate.

VII

Which body was yours?

You were a girl, but also a man.
A man to father children.

The body can't decide.

The hips front, but the foot
reverts to stars:
flesh before the flesh,
the freeze and drag.

Then the cough, and wetness in the bed.

VIII

Ab: a syllable dipped
in two thoughts,
conscious and unconscious.
Back to back, Freud said;
their spines aswirl.

So the phrase
I didn't think of that
becomes a bookend: furniture
for the dim and breathing room.

In years to come, it might rise
in a double helix,
necklaced as DNA.

IX

The old woman's lips were on mine
that night. The kiss said,
You can shred yourself
to make another:
your self is now enough
for an anchor and a wing.

Someone loves the all of you:
if he comes home to find you gone,
he'll be lost in some other country.

X

In early spring, scilla is a raft
in the grass.

As Scylla in the rock would stay the sailors.

Violent delft:
the work of a steaming pool.

And then the blue that surfaces in Padua,
wells behind the crowds within the fresco:
the ether
behind the haloed heads.

Heaven is a hole within the old dream
of luster and perimeter.

(The *lustre,* I heard you say: the chandelier.)

XI *Vienna Waltzes*

As couples mill
beneath electric evergreens,
a woman catches up her skirts
with one hand—
a semaphore!—
and slowly,
she begins to dance alone.

We watch the deep
bend of her knees
before each storied rise.

A mirror doubles the whirl
until her skirts
dervish.

She curtsies and then arches,
her bare back in muscular
mosaic:

so beautiful is the skeleton, the symptom.

XII

I saw through a clouded reticle—

the populace of language underneath.

A still pool, the interlocking words

murmured again by you, by the doctor.

You were tired, from the wish to be one.

You floated, yet thirsted for an edge—

your body always falling into ether.

The white sheet is cross-hatched,

the bed like a transparency;

or membranes of *somniferum:*

vellum, to be written on.

III

Restoration:
The Senses

Cicadas

for Lisa Petrie

Their sound is metallic,
as you say: a hum
nearly industrial,
since every noise in nature
is also necessarily
historical;

and here in Illinois,
where they sing or solder
all the August day,
their notes mark time
in quick or labored
crescendos.

Here on the prairie,
I'm counting
on the telephone
for words.
And when you laugh
and describe

cicadas you heard
thirty years ago
by the bay,
I hear them better
than the sound
that now

lines my living room
like silver,
like steel:
what else
do you remember
so sharply?

And if that caliber
of memory
is in you, what else
can we ever
mean by *secrets*
when we listen

to each other
for hours, like girls?
I want to restore
the particles
that formed us
before we met:

dune striations,
or the toll
of grace notes
in church songs—all
the stucco
and the gold.

I know that in the last days,
all I'll have is memory:
so, yes, I'll need
the milkweed,
the hairstyle, all the wet
eidetic leaves—

to take with me
when I wade
without you
through summer grass
grown taller
than my sight.

Seeing In

I'm grateful for the way my eye travels—
or skirts, looping over canvas, hillsides smooth
and spackled as walls; I'm grateful for the farmhouse
troweled on green foundations, its replica
half-vanished in the grass, my eye cutting spirals

on the surface: school figures, early morning ice;
I'm grateful that oils compound and shimmer
in museum light, but only when I lean in closer
and rest my eye mothlike on a slip of blue burning
under brown, accreted like bow strokes

trellising a fugue, or *andante* moving
with the urgency of paradox; I'm grateful for unrest
under colors, for all I need to rove
to see, for fields of vision populous as fields.

The New Retina

is little more
than a sequin
in the doctor's palm,

dull as sterling spoons
passed among
generations,

but magic as the chip
or the quark,
promising
to net the world

for this man,
who returned
from the war
and married,

and felt a fog
filtering the faces
in the pews.

Years later,
he's forgotten
the shape
of his daughter's eyes,

though he'd guess
her forehead's low
and broad
as his own.

If he could,
he'd ask the doctor
for perimeter—

not the vein's
streak, the changes
in the hair:

the landmarks
he remembers
are adobe
or paper,

like the strips
her scissors made
years ago:

doll legs,
two short arms—

he wants to say
at his age,
he's through
with the scintillant,

the sealing
of spirit
over dirt:

what would he do
with light
dappled frantic
on water,

a girl swaddled
back to him
as nimbus,

all her edges
given up
the ghost?

Inventions

I. Psalm Invention in the West

Bach's Two-Part Invention no. 2 in C minor

If I were to shimmer in a pool in the canyon
If afternoon rain burned the gem that is water
If precipitation pooled as lapis in the slick rock
Encrusted westward in a turtle's shell
Stippled painted in the world not for us

If a maidenhair fern were reflected there
Effaced by the cloud's hand, arabesque and index
Anaphora in the rocks over the pool
If my body were broken in the fault
If a reed thins to music and fractures and repairs

If I followed   If I leapt across the rock
If I listened hard to your voice without music
If it spoke to me *cantabile*   If I followed
If the paintbrush pooled   If you carried me down
If the two of us rappelled to sea level

II. *Arc Away*

Bach's Two-Part Invention no. 7 in E minor

Love is bad
brio: why
do you stoke
its adrenaline
engine, its humming-

bird emblem
all microscopic
motor, indigo
dispersing
in a whirl: do you see

how hysteria
trumps hue?
How the heart
has sublimed
the wings,

eaten every instinct
for solitary
distances? A bird
should arc
away, not

hover there
ex machina,
plumb above
the runoff, creature
evaporate and still:

do you hear
his motor humming
like a stone?
Are you
sand-blind?

What ails you?
The vanishing
point burns,
beckoning
and blue.

III. *Green World*

Bach's Two-Part Invention no. 12 in A major,
played by Glenn Gould

When it's stiller,
you can hear his voice
tinkering behind
the notes: hammering,
truing, as he dammed
or corked the instrument;
now, though, his cup
runneth over
as in all the Clear
Creeks of the west;
trout are pirouetting
from the water,
then writing on the air;
sunflowers arc
their coppers and darks
in swaths
articulate as digital
photography: can these
be the imprints
of our new
imaginations?
Where is joy
but in these silken
bolts of rhetoric,
indelicate
turnings of hyperbole?

Saussure and the Divers

Synchronized diving
Athens, 2004

By all accounts,
he was interested
in synchrony,
the foliate
rather than the seed;
but would he then
have measured
the lines of the pike,
the moment
the foreheads
graze the knees,
or the smallness
two somersaults achieve
before the twin divers
nose the water, sharing
the merest,
softest splash?
The better divers know
to divest themselves
of cumber, shearing
the body from its fodder,
rippling down the live wire
ironing out their fingers
to their toes—
sinking, then,
with the dignity
of syntax spent;

he, on the other hand,
kept driving
his own lone
bumper car of language—
synchronous, yes,
but in the way
of shooting
marbles, or anagrams
that swim up
in a book;
he learned that language
was not *of the garment;*
it is that of the train
and the street:
cut cloth is never
an idiom in bloom,
though crowds of top hats
line a street
new with industry,
its pediments
skirted in scaffolding—
and then he learned
to look out long
and name the constellations
in his hand:
dragonfly,
pumpkin, cat's-eye.

The Desk

Near the end
of the somersault,
the wings
skirt like crinoline:
a slip flares

before the two
points sheathe;
as the dancer's leg
whips into *fouetté,*
clicks as a gear,

so the beetle
realigns, again
pedestrian,
to rove the lamp's
light stem.

Windy City

They wrote all over the rocks, the ones
who came before and come still; choicer
than graffiti, the paint cubed and letters
blocked like epitaphs: *Acid* or *small groove*
or *baby cakes.* And primary colors whet
the schools of foam the lake makes,
its mobile cursive less serene, while the city
wells above that trace of sociability—
its steeples snuffed, or nearly, in the mist:
this could have been Christminster,
or these the moral rocks Tess read
on her journey home in terrible,
delicate boots: the shores mirror us
always, but the city transpires.

Pond Way

Just as he once said
*The forest was my first
art lesson,* so
his laptop

stirred this pond,
made his dancers
dance; with Life Forms,
Cunningham partnered
the cool screen,

trained the wire
pliés of the virtual,
who dance
as virtuosos,
with no pain:

the first pond steps,
his strings
of rough and tumble,
were danced
onscreen without

footfall: *I put it on
the slowest speed,
to see if
I can add
something:*

2

onstage, each dancer
has four arms,
four legs:

a loose silk strip
loops shoulder
to wrist,
knee to ankle,

so the body's weight
evaporates
as plush;

so, as in water,
each straight arm
is phantom-bent;

in *attitude,* the woman
lifts her face
to another:

a mirror, a sliver
of inference.

Free Throw

His face, behind the curving line,
is white. Or black.
A smooth plate
of forehead on him.
His large shoes
pigeon-toe, as if
he's playing hopscotch
alone, his teammates
loping and dispersing
as he dribbles—
and just before his hands
lift above his head,
you'll see a flash
of Adam's wrath,
some one-on-Atlas-
one, all the stories
older than TV: Job's cry
as one dancer
danced it,
his furiously
flagging spine
storming the creator.

Helve

Do they feel good in your hands?
he asked, as I turned
a fork and knife,
traced a spoon's
dim basin:
as if we bought silver
with our palms
alone, scored to gauge
small metal
terrains: to test
scars scrawled in steel,
acanthus sprouting tines—
as if our very fingertips
elicit a helve,
our cells' ambition realized
in mason work
or Braille: the machine
of two hands
fanning from the seam.

Malibu Lipstick

Who would wear
darkest mulberry
on snow, on rice
powder, don the perennial
startle of the Noh mask (carved
and painted balsam pine),
its clear temple folded
like paper?—Who would choose
ivory skin anathema
to beaches, to running
in the sun's light:
to duck the torch
and tallow
of its scorch?

Malibu lipstick
is wax stain
on orchids, hot
pigment dolloped
thio-indigo, pooled
on the mouth
below the tendriled
Phalaenopsis
antennae, ur-lure
of tentacle
and sloe: but no
mouth—no countenance,
no wants.

Rue Family

O, you must wear your rue with a difference.

—SHAKESPEARE, *HAMLET*

April makes no difference
to the Lavalle cork tree
imported from central Japan;

to the Sakhalin cork,
its diamond bark
rising into branches

from a trunk of plated sand.
In the city park, this family of trees
wears its rue as buds

traveled into leaf each year—
predictably, invisibly
as your sister wears hers

on a South Dakota highway:
there behind her knee; tempering
the air above her hand.

Falconer

Near the slaking gray of the sea,
a kite braids up,
the flag
of a private country:

Ben, do you want to fly?

And the boy steps up
to the sandy plate,
as if he knows
when to reel, when
to let the wind
helter-skelter—
digging in
to steady the skyline,

falconing a shore's
weight in flutter:
the streaming bird
parts cirrus
from low tide,
testing the glass
of the built world.

Mercurial (Soap, Glass, Skull)

I

He's too old for soap bubbles,
but still the boy leans from the sill
into the dark, his lips' duct lofting
a porous ellipse about to break,
his face quiet as a room lit
by a single lamp; and from where I sit,
that light has scrubbed his temple
to a shard—so I hold my breath
and try to read the bubble's
book of blank, lifting to stay
for a moment, perhaps two,
in the air: the boy learning
to exhale, not sing,
his ceremony solemn
as Latin declensions, as paper
flowering in pools: the grindstone
and vertigo of art.

II

In the factory,
men twirl wands
until the blues
spool and mound:

threads
of hot glass dip
and craze into forms.

Tongs pull a leg,
then a leg
from a liquid

torso, soon
to harden as a horse.

And now a seer
takes to the woods, parting
a branch to make his dream:

four men row a boat
to the darkest
region of the sea.

One looks up
and sees a flock of crows
stilled above him.

III

If I ever said I loved you,
which I probably
won't, the words might sound
like a pipe
posed under glass,
or a map of some near galaxy:
planets shrubbed
in deepening green,
cress lit
by a starburst
of impulse—

this window box
an artist called
Dream World.

IV

There's a bubble housed
in the pediment above the skull;
it floats above the frazzle
in the bone.

Then a river of coins
you can never spend:
the balance
of cranium from gable.

The last transformation
is the one
you'll never see:

the lesson is inlaid with gold.

One Thousand Cranes

"Flying Geese," pieced quilt (ca. 1845–50)

In those days, a couple went to bed with geese—
eight hundred and twenty-six triangles
flown northward in calico, each bird pared
to wingspread and a compass-point of head.

There was a terrain that held them at a distance:
root and tumbleweed stenciled in the chintz
that pieced the unmarked trail beneath their feathers;
sparks of earth that fell away from bird's eye, marrying

geometry and spores—like our digital cameras'
fort-da, or sudden willows grown behind the blinds
of my youngest childhood home in the Midwest.
The cloth tracks are running distant as brooks

seen from the locked towers of dream,
while isosceles rush over the plains' surface,
no shape cut from the same dress or drape:
the triangles are lace, or a tangle of bike spokes;

or three points fence the scalloped
edges of Corinthians. And now her body
stirs beneath the cloth. *Let me see a triangle of sky,*
she told him, *right before I die.* But I think that voice

belongs to a woman who lives here now,
who also asked her husband for the possible:
to watch a stream of birds migrate
on the television propped above her bed;

to return to the seat of her oldest ideas,
where a thousand cranes glide in a girl's
silk pocket: mathematical, sublime, and small—
she almost feels the wings against her hip.

I Had No Human Fears

So one day you look
and the door's
ajar: reeling in
the years, those songs

break new—public now
as a herd stopped
at a stone
wall; and no one's there

who took the hand
of Whitman—
let them stream on
the media: *how many*

vacation days do you
have left;
let them say
a slumber did,

and then erase the *s*
from *spirit;*
every Sunday,
I read stacks

of mail
asking how
to leave this world
when we can't;

asking for language
like a burr,
like a spell—
I want to write them all

and say
don't rest—
don't rest;
and think of the ones

who never had
the dawning: the slit
throats of the two
girls in Zion.

Lineage

This book's a hand-me-down
from a friend I only speak to
nowadays in dreams,
when my questions rise
like smoke from a departing train
and she turns her head
too late to answer me.

On the cover, a line drawing
of a ravine and trees.
An inscription, "To Phil,"
from the poet, inside:
my friend's older brother
was the book's first owner,
before he left to study Spanish
in New Orleans.

For years, Phil's sister
has stayed mum in California,
though she said lost friends
grow back like limbs
when you need them most.

I turn the book over.
The poet sets his chin
against hardwood.

I've eaten his vowels for breakfast,
breathed his blanks
like the cleanest air.

I want to talk and talk to that face,
to trace the branching
of my own questions.

I Shall Not Want

Restoration: listen
to the temple
in the word, the sound
that convalesces—
the dark clothes
radiate, strewn
with lilies.

The sound of the screw
is gentle, suited
to the ancient
tinker, so the hole
in the ring
receives its ruby;

or workers swab
the sapphire
wash behind the fresco,
cobalt oxide, soil
for the haloes
sown in furrows;

even the skeleton
allium in winter
restores, silvertint,
its sphere of points
eternally unblossomed:

and how, then,
to zero out the losses,
to gather
the prairie back
in armloads

so your lost
breast, ghosted
in cirrus,
will float
free of the X-ray's zoom—

Repent

for Linda Barker

I saw it first in the light
of erasure:
he'd painted a thicket
over an angel, here
where the corner
of the forest
condenses,

where I can smell
the juniper,
its scent of *pentimento:*
penitence, I hear,
in the painting over;

and then I watched a finch
pooling in the bush,
threading
the lattice
of its feathers—

and there beneath
your hand's flight,
I saw the silted halo
refracted as leaves, laying
a wall of introspection,

faith grown
like brambles in the windows;

and then the wake
of your hand
in the museum—

you, mapped
by the frames' path;

and the finch
among us, belated
and waiting.

ABOUT THE AUTHOR

Christina Pugh is a recipient of the Lucille Medwick Memorial Award from the Poetry Society of America, the Grolier Poetry Prize, and a fellowship in poetry from the Illinois Arts Council. She is also the author of *Rotary*, which was awarded the 2003 Word Press First Book Prize, and the chapbook *Gardening at Dusk*. Her poems and reviews have appeared in journals, including the *Atlantic Monthly, Harvard Review*, and *Poetry*. Pugh is an assistant professor in the Program for Writers at the University of Illinois at Chicago. She lives in Evanston, Illinois.